TRUTH
AND
HONOR

The President Ford Story

LINDSEY McDIVITT ★ Illustrated by MATT FAULKNER

 PUBLISHED BY SLEEPING BEAR PRESS

President Gerald R. Ford sat down at his new desk in the Oval Office and rolled up his sleeves, ready for work. He'd never planned to be president, but Ford was just the leader America needed. He would help mend what was broken—the trust between the people and their government.

Americans would see their new president could be counted on to tell the truth. Honest and hardworking, he followed the rules. He cared deeply about all Americans. Gerald Ford could steer them through the turbulence of recent events. His life had prepared him well.

Plus, Liberty was at his side. . . .

"I believe that truth is the glue that holds government together, not only our Government but civilization itself."

GERALD R. FORD, JR.
REMARKS UPON BEING SWORN IN AS PRESIDENT OF THE UNITED STATES,
AUGUST 9, 1974

As a baby in 1913, Junior, as he was called back then, survived stormy times. His mother, Dorothy, escaped her violent husband by clutching her baby close and slipping out the door without even a suitcase. Dorothy fled Omaha, Nebraska, to her parents, with Junior, then just 16 days old. They all moved to Grand Rapids, Michigan, to start a new life.

Dorothy remarried when Junior was too small to recall the father they'd left behind. Now he had a stepfather—Gerald Ford, an honorable man, as dependable as the lighthouse shining at Grand Haven beach.

As Junior grew, his stepfather threw footballs to him and took him fishing. Gerald Senior became the father Junior loved. The new family grew close and Junior tried to follow his parents' three rules—"tell the truth, work hard, and come to dinner on time."

Junior found lessons to be learned from those close to him.

From his stepfather, Junior learned to be hardworking and honest—to play by the rules.

From his mother, he learned to think of others, and to study hard. And to control his hot temper—most of the time.

From the people of Grand Rapids, good neighbors and friends—Junior Ford learned to respect many kinds of people, including those new to America.

The Great Depression hit and hardships buffeted the Fords. Business was bad at his family's paint store and they lost their home to the bank. But the Fords found joy all around them. Joy as deep and vast as the Great Lakes ringing their state.

Junior raced down Ottawa beach with his little brothers. He and his stepfather trolled for trout on the Pere Marquette River. Mother's cooking and happy spirit brought them together for dinner.

Before long, Junior was given the same name as the stepfather he admired. Junior became known as "Gerald with a G, but Jerry with a J."

But still, life sometimes felt like being caught in a whirlwind. In school, young Jerry hoped the teacher wouldn't call on him. Although he was smart, he struggled to speak. And left-handed Jerry was expected to write with his right hand. He tried and tried, until finally teachers stopped forcing him. Once he was allowed to be different and write with his left hand, Jerry's stuttering stopped.

Working multiple jobs to help out his family, Jerry learned to get things done.

He mixed colors and cleaned out vats at his stepfather's paint store.

He hefted crates of sodas and Cracker Jacks at an amusement park.

He washed dirty dishes and waited on lunch customers at Bill's Place.

Jerry attended public high school where students strived to succeed through hard work—no matter where they came from or the color of their skin. The desire for the American Dream flowed through the school as strongly as the Grand River flowed through town.

Jerry's stepdad believed "sports taught you how to live, how to compete, but always by the rules." And Jerry dove into sports with gusto—slicing through the water as a swimmer, racing down the track or basketball court, and tackling players on the football field.

With his Boy Scout troop, Jerry spent time in the wilderness and helping his community. As an Eagle Scout, he was one of the first chosen to serve as Honor Guard at the fort on Mackinac Island.

His efforts made his mother proud.

From the Boy Scouts, he learned patriotism and to be of service to others.

From sports, he learned teamwork and how to follow the rules of the game.

And from fellow students, Jerry learned what it meant to struggle and strive.

Jerry made plans for college. His future looked as bright as the Dutch tulips that decorated his city. But dark clouds loomed during the Great Depression. Millions searched for work. Jerry's stepdad took less money home so he could keep all his workers on the job. His mother volunteered collecting food for people in need. The Fords felt fortunate, but there was no money for college.

So Jerry worked harder. Two jobs washing dishes on campus, plus a $100 gift from his high school, covered Jerry's tuition and expenses at the University of Michigan in Ann Arbor.

He made the football team—playing home games in the enormous new stadium. On road trips Jerry and his new buddy, Willis Ward, were roommates. Back then many hotels would not permit African Americans to stay as guests, so before away games, their coach called ahead—demanding Willis be allowed in with the team.

Teams from the South often refused to share the field with black players. In 1934, Willis was forced to sit out a home game against Georgia Tech.

Jerry had a temper—usually under control—but now he was angry. Furious. He wrestled with what to do. Should he refuse to play? Or quit the team altogether?

Making this decision was more difficult than scaling the steep dunes on the shores of Lake Michigan. He sought out advice and listened hard. He wrote to his stepfather. He spoke more with his coach. And he talked to Willis. "The team needs you," said Willis. You should play, go pound them for me, he told Jerry.

Reluctantly Jerry played, and Michigan won. But he never forgot that ugly lesson.

After college Jerry turned down offers to play professional football. His goal was law school. Again, there was no money, so Jerry felt lucky to get coaching jobs at Yale University in Connecticut.

> ## "*The harder you work, the better your luck.*"
>
> GERALD FORD SR., JERRY'S STEPFATHER

At first Yale wouldn't let him into their prestigious law classes, but Jerry kept pushing until he had his degree. Graduating with impressive grades, he declined jobs with big firms and packed his bags for Grand Rapids. First he'd open his own law office, and then he was thinking of running for Congress.

But while driving home from his office on December 7, 1941, Jerry's radio blared the news—Japanese planes had attacked Pearl Harbor. Jerry knew his duty. When America declared war on Japan, he volunteered for the Navy. On the aircraft carrier *Monterey*, Jerry was barraged by storms and battles at sea.

One night, an enormous typhoon hit. Sirens sounded and Jerry rushed to the deck as huge waves rocked the ship. He was thrown down—sliding toward the roiling sea. Almost too late, Jerry caught the tiny deck edge with his feet . . . and saved himself.

Grateful to return to the peaceful fields and forests of Michigan, Jerry wanted to help people—beginning with those in his home state. Michigan badly needed an honest worker in government, much as its orchards needed rain and sunshine. So Jerry campaigned in Grand Rapids for the United States Congress.

From college and law school, he'd learned to listen, to both sides. And to seek out the best advice.

From coaching, he'd learned leadership, and how to encourage teamwork.

From fighting to free other nations, he'd learned how important American democracy was to peace and justice worldwide.

In 1949, Michigan voters sent Jerry to the House of Representatives. People in his district trusted that he heard their concerns and would speak up for them. With his new bride, Betty, he moved to Washington, D.C.

"You are a person of your word . . . the integrity of your word . . . is a tremendous possession of great value. Keep it. Never lose it."

GERALD FORD SR., JERRY'S STEPFATHER

Harry Truman was the first of six presidents Jerry Ford worked with as a Republican congressman. Jerry believed the political parties were on the same team. He became known for working with the Democrats, bridging the gap the way the Mackinac Bridge connects Michigan's peninsulas.

"As far as I'm concerned, there are no enemies in politics — just temporary opponents who might vote with you on the next Roll Call."

GERALD R. FORD JR., UPON RECEIVING THE JOHN F. KENNEDY
PROFILE IN COURAGE AWARD, MAY 21, 2001

During his 25 years in Congress, Gerald Ford's votes supported the rights of Americans—all religions, genders, abilities, and colors—he never forgot the racism that hurt his friend Willis in college. And Jerry never stopped listening to the people of Michigan.

"*We hold these truths to be self-evident, that all men are created equal, that they are endowed by their Creator with certain unalienable Rights, that among these are Life, Liberty and the pursuit of Happiness.*"

THE DECLARATION OF INDEPENDENCE

In the 1970s the country faced a flood of bad news. Both the president and vice president were accused of breaking the law, and lying about it. Protesters marched, demanding the truth.

Vice President Agnew was forced to leave his job. President Nixon needed a new vice president. One who followed the rules. One who people trusted. He selected Jerry Ford.

Jerry knew there was a chance President Nixon might be found guilty of his crimes. Then he, Gerald Ford, would become president of the United States.

The events of 1974 rocked the nation. President Nixon was forced to leave office, and Gerald R. Ford became the 38th president of the United States. "We can do it. We are ready," Jerry told Betty, who was by now a trusted helpmate.

"We will have an open . . . candid administration. I can't change my nature after 61 years."

PRESIDENT GERALD R. FORD

Jerry's new desk was piled high with problems. New storms threatened. The war in Vietnam was ending and Jerry wanted to help the thousands of refugees who were now in need of a country to call home. There were fears of another depression. People worried about paying for food, gasoline, and housing.

But now Americans had a president they could trust working for them—a president with integrity. And Jerry knew how to navigate tough times and make the right choices. He knew how to learn from those around him, to look out for others. He knew how to lead.

President Ford would do his very best to steer the country to safety. They were all in this together. And Gerald R. Ford was a strong captain at the helm.

"My fellow Americans, our long national nightmare is over. Our Constitution works; our great Republic is a government of laws and not of men. Here the people rule."

PRESIDENT GERALD R. FORD, PUBLIC REMARKS FOLLOWING TAKING THE OATH OF OFFICE AS PRESIDENT, AUGUST 9, 1974

Dear Young Readers,

Being the children of the president of the United States was pretty special. We were able to meet celebrities and heads of state, travel to neat places, and run around in the White House with our dog, Liberty. Yes, we had some wonderful opportunities as members of the First Family, but the greatest experience was seeing firsthand the roles our dad played: a loving husband and father, a compassionate public servant and friend to his fellow citizens, and an honorable and courageous leader of our nation.

As you have read, our dad faced many personal and professional challenges and disappointments from his early years all the way through his later life as president. Those hardships taught our Dad the lessons that made him the man he became and prepared him for the roles he would play for our family and the nation. Through these setbacks, our dad learned the value of hard work, how to persevere in the face of adversity, the importance of telling the truth, and how to care for and lead those also facing struggles.

These life lessons from our dad (and mom) were a great encouragement and inspiration to us as their children. But the greatest gift that they gave to each of us was their unconditional love and acceptance of us as good and valuable people, even when we made our share of mistakes.

We are very grateful to Lindsey McDivitt, Matt Faulkner, and the many folks at Sleeping Bear Press for writing and illustrating this true and compelling story of our dad's life and legacy. We hope that in reading his story, you too will understand the gift of our dad's life to the many people who he touched, loved, and served.

We wish you the very best in your own journey of growth, development, and service to others.

Mike, Jack, Steve, and Susan Ford

President Gerald R. Ford Timeline

1913

Gerald R. Ford is born as Leslie Lynch King Jr. in Omaha, Nebraska, to Leslie and Dorothy King.

1917

Dorothy King marries Gerald R. Ford Sr. in Grand Rapids, Michigan.

1927-1931

Ford attends South High School in Grand Rapids. He excels at football and is named to the All-City and All-State teams.

1934

Michigan beats Georgia Tech 9-2, despite Willis Ward being sidelined for the football game. Ford enjoyed a lifelong friendship with Ward, who became a Detroit probate judge.

1935

Ford declines professional football offers from the Green Bay Packers and the Detroit Lions.

1935

December 3— He legally changes his name to Gerald R. Ford Jr.

1942-1946

Ford serves with distinction in the U.S. Navy during World War II.

1948

October 15—Gerald R. Ford Jr. and Elizabeth (Betty) Bloomer Warren marry.

November 2—Ford is elected to his first term as a U.S. congressman. He is reelected 12 times and serves from 1949 to 1973.

1949-1964

Congressman Ford supports many efforts to desegregate schools, gain equal pay for equal work by women, and protect employment and voting rights for people of color.

1950-1957

The Fords welcome the birth of their children: Michael, John (Jack), Steven, and Susan.

1964

Ford votes for the Civil Rights Act outlawing employment discrimination based on race, color, religion, sex, or national origin.

1965

Ford leads Republicans in passing the Voting Rights Act to protect people of color from efforts to take away their right to vote.

1968

November 5—Richard M. Nixon is elected president with Spiro Agnew as vice president.

1973

December 6—Ford replaces Agnew as vice president; this is the first use of the 25th Amendment.

1974

August 8—President Richard M. Nixon announces his plan to resign, believing he will be impeached and convicted after his role in the Watergate break-in is made public.

August 9—Gerald R. Ford takes the oath of office to become the 38th American president.

September—Ford officially pardons Richard Nixon, avoiding a long trial. This angers many, but he believes strongly that the nation must begin to heal. As president he needs to focus on other problems and reestablish America's leadership in the world.

1975

Following America's exit from the Vietnam War, President Ford organizes the airlift of almost 120,000 Vietnamese refugees to safety in the United States.

August 26—This day is declared as Women's Equality Day by President Ford, who long supported the Equal Rights Amendment.

1975

September—There are two attempts to assassinate President Ford.

1977

January 7—Gerald Ford leaves the office of president after a close election with Jimmy Carter.

1981

The Ford Presidential Library and Museum are dedicated.

2000

September—The University of Michigan in Ann Arbor celebrates renaming their School of Public Policy after President Gerald R. Ford. Henry Kissinger delivers the keynote address.

2006

December 26—President Gerald R. Ford dies at age 93.

For my mom and dad with gratitude for this life in America
L.M.

Dedicated to our children — Joe, Julia & Gabriel
and to my Kris, always
M.J.

SLEEPING BEAR PRESS™

BRINGING MEANINGFUL
STORIES TO YOUNG READERS